OFF-KEY PRAISES

OFF-KEY PRAISES

*Second Thoughts
on
Scripture Texts*

JOHN STRIETELMEIER

CONCORDIA PUBLISHING HOUSE

Concordia Publishing House, St. Louis, Missouri
Concordia Publishing House Ltd., London, E. C. 1
© 1968 Concordia Publishing House
Library of Congress Catalog Card No. 68—13893

MANUFACTURED IN THE UNITED STATES OF AMERICA

To the memory of Elizabeth Ruth
Looman, 1958—1967

PREFACE

Man's noblest work is to adore his God. It may be that, in doing this work, one can perform some useful service to his brothers and sisters in the faith. But whether he does so or not, he has at least made his own act of worship and he may hope that his off-key praises contribute something to that joyful noise which the whole creation is bound, by duty and by gratitude, to make to its Lord.

It is my conviction that the only proper source and ground of Christian praise is the revelation of His nature and His works which God has given us in the Holy Scriptures. The subtitle of this book, "Second Thoughts on Scripture Texts," is, therefore, a confession of plagiarism. My second thoughts claim to be no more than echoes of the first thoughts of those men of God through whom He chose to make Himself known to successive generations of the faithful. I hope that no one will look for—much less find—anything "original" in this book. Those who have a hankering for something original in matters of theology will have no difficulty finding it in any number of books which have appeared in our age of multiplying heresies.

JOHN STRIETELMEIER
Valparaiso University

CONTENTS

Off-Key Praise
ROMANS 11:33-36

There was an eccentric Englishman in the 19th century who objected to a large part of Christian worship on the grounds that "no gentleman cares to be praised to his face." The assumption that God is a gentleman is one that might be questioned, but the idea that Christian worship is a kind of exercise in flattering God is one that has to be denied.

God does not need our praise, and indeed we are not able to praise Him as we ought. We need to praise God, for as one of our hymns puts it, "Your noblest work is to adore." Man is a creature, and when the creature stands before his Creator, he cannot merely stare at Him like some dumb animal and keep silence. Even in his sin, man knows that perfection is praiseworthy, and in the presence of the Holy God even His enemies cannot but sing praises.

Christian people, of course, have even more reason to praise God, for they know Him not only as their Creator but also as their Redeemer; not only as the sublime, mysterious Holy Trinity but also as the God whose name is Love. He does not have to command our praises. He has to exercise His love and patience to listen to the poor, off-key praise that wells up out of our hearts onto lisping, stam-

9

mering tongues which are simply not adequate for the great task of praising Him.

It is not God who is flattered, therefore, by our praises. It is He who flatters us by listening, by prompting us when we know that we must speak but don't know what to say, and by never even hinting that the very best we bring Him is really pretty bad.

Peace Be Unto You
JOHN 20:19-23

When our Lord appeared to His disciples after His resurrection, the greeting He brought them was a familiar one—"Peace be unto you!" But on His lips it carried a whole world of new meaning. What other men could speak only as a wish or a prayer, He could speak as a benediction, for by His death and resurrection He had become the Prince of Peace, and peace was His to give to His people.

Thus it was with our Lord. He brought nothing new, and yet He made all things new. Bread and wine had sustained man's physical life as far back as human records go; but when He blessed them they became His body and blood, food to sustain the souls of His people. Water had been used from earliest times to cleanse and purify; His

Word gave it power to wash away sin. Jews for centuries had greeted each other with "Peace be unto you"; He raised the greeting to the level of God's own word of forgiveness.

It is this sanctification of the ordinary that many people find offensive in Christianity. The Christian faith is not "spiritual" enough for them. Bread, wine, water, words—are these the only weapons God has to rout His enemies and rescue His people? Where is the sign from heaven? Where is the New Thing that men can take as 100 percent proof that this Man was God, Lord, and Savior?

"Peace be unto you!" The Lord Christ is found in the common and the familiar. Until Jesus came, the words meant little more than "Hello." On His lips—and on ours when we speak in His name—they mean, "Be of good cheer. Thy sins be forgiven thee."

For Men of Little Faith

MATTHEW 6:24-34

It is probably not just coincidental that what some people have called our "post-Christian age" has been called by others an "age of anxiety." Man has always demanded an answer to the question: "Is the universe friendly?" And the least satisfactory answer anyone can give him is: "I don't know."

Jesus Christ, the Son of God, by whom all things were made, knew the answer to that question. It was and is "Yes," for the God whom He taught His followers to address in prayer is not some vague First Cause or some unapproachable Brilliance in a far-off heaven, but our Father. And like a father pities his children, so our Father pities those who fear Him.

And this concern is not limited to "spiritual" matters. Our Father takes a lively, personal interest in everything that affects the happiness and well-being of His children—their health, their budget, their needs for food and clothing and shelter, their courtships and marriages, their jobs, their hopes and ambitions. We may hesitate to bring these concerns to our Father because they are not "religious" enough; but He makes them His business nevertheless, for He is God, and God is Love.

Anxiety therefore is a demonstration of little faith. When we are paralyzed by worry or fear, we are saying one of two things: either we do not believe God really cares, or we do not believe He will help us. If we say the first, we make Him a liar. If we say the second, we make Him a devil—for a God who knows our needs and can help us but won't is not Love but the very incarnation of evil.

Your heavenly Father knows that you have need of all these things. Why, then, are you fearful, O you of little faith?

God Is Love

1 JOHN 4:16-21

One doesn't have to be a Christian to know much that is true about God. The Hindu confesses: "Thou art the father of this world. There is no peer to thee, O king beyond likeness." An ancient Chinese poem includes these lines: "Great Heaven is intelligent. And is with you in all your goings. Great Heaven is clear-seeing. And is with you in your wanderings and indulgences." The Moslem prays: "Blessed be God, Lord of the worlds! The compassionate, the merciful! King on the day of reckoning!"

But only the Christian knows the full truth about God, and he knows it only because God Himself has told him. God is Love! Imagine—the God who made and rules this world, in which millions of people never get enough to eat, in which children are born with cerebral palsy, in which madmen plunge whole nations into war—this God is Love!

If the eternal and unchangeable God really is Love, then obviously all of these unlovely and unloving things which we see about us in the world and in our own lives cannot last. Indeed, we ourselves cannot last as we are. We must be changed, so radically remade that eventually each one of us can say of himself, as God says of Himself, "I am love."

This change takes place in Baptism, and it is repeated every day of our lives as we drown the old evil, selfish nature within us and put on the righteousness of Christ which God gives us in the forgiveness of sins. This righteousness is complete. Dressed in Jesus' blood and righteousness we pass safely through the deep waters of death and stand triumphant before the throne of God.

Sure As the Promises of God
JOHN 14:15-20

Can God be trusted?

When this question is asked in church on a Sunday morning, everybody knows what the answer is supposed to be, and it comes out loud and clear: "Of course He can be trusted. How could God break His word?"

But ask that question in the middle of a hectic week, at the end of a hard day, at the height of a family quarrel, or at any moment during the long night before surgery, and the answer is neither loud nor clear. "Can God be trusted? I don't know. I hope so, but I am not really sure. Can God love me when I hate myself? Can He forgive me when I find it impossible to forgive myself? Can He really want me to live with Him forever when I can hardly stand to live with myself?"

When these questions arise, there is only one thing to do: remember what promises have been made to you and who made them. You believe that the paper money in your billfold is good, even though it is nothing more than a promise to pay. You count on your life insurance, but your policy is only as good as the company that wrote it. Is God as trustworthy as the Treasurer of the United States or your life insurance company?

If He is — and He is — take Him at His word and believe that He really means it when He says: "I have loved thee with an everlasting love, I have called thee by My name, thou art Mine. No man shall pluck thee out of My hand. I will not leave thee comfortless. I will come again and receive you unto Myself. Where I am, there shalt thou be also."

Every Good and Perfect Gift
JAMES 1:16-21

With God, says St. James, there is no "variation or shadow due to change." This means simply that God is consistent, that He is dependable, that He doesn't get moody or temperamental as we do.

If we believe that God is good at all, we must believe that He is always good. If we believe that anything He sent into our lives was good, we must believe that everything He sends us is good. For God is not just another name for luck—sometimes good and sometimes bad. God is God—the same yesterday, and today, and forever.

Christians have no need, therefore, of horoscopes or tea leaves or wishing wells. All that one needs to know—or, for that matter, can know—about the future is that the unchanging God will still be there and that He will still be sending down His good and perfect gifts.

Is there really "no variation or shadow due to change" with the good and gracious God? If so, then everything that we fear in the future is His good and perfect gift—the unexpected expense, the sudden hospitalization, the loss of friends and loved ones, our own death.

This is easy to say. It is much harder to believe. And what makes it especially hard to believe is that we know all too well how we would act if we were in God's place. We know how we would handle the kind of people we are. But God cannot be mean or petty. He can only be what He is.

And as long as He is what He is, all things must work together for good to those who love Him, even those things which look like anything but good and perfect gifts from above.

He Cares for You
1 PETER 5:6-11

Deep down inside all of us lurks a stubborn pride that insists on keeping something to ourselves — something that is strictly "our own business," nobody else's, not even God's. For many of us this something is our troubles.

"Sure, I take my big problems to God," we say. "I wouldn't know where else to turn for forgiveness or for healing in a major illness or for comfort at the death of a loved one. But why should I bother Him with a lot of little things? I ought to handle these things myself without running to God for help. After all, God has this whole great universe to run. Why should He care about this little toothache or this shaky bank balance of mine?"

Why should He care? That is His secret and He has not chosen to share it with us. But whatever His reasons may be, He does care for us and He wants us to bring Him not only our big problems but also those little, nagging irritations that spoil our days and sour our dispositions. He wants us to cast *all* our care on Him.

"Well," we say, "if I ran to God with every little ache and pain I never would learn to stand on my own feet. I would become completely dependent on God." And, for once, we would be right. We would be doing precisely what St. Peter tells us to do: By casting all our care upon God, we would be humbling ourselves under the mighty hand of God. We would stop talking nonsense about "standing on our own two feet," which is just another way of saying that we want to be junior-grade gods, and we would be admitting our complete dependence on God.

This is precisely what it means to believe in God.

The Lord, Our Rock

1 CORINTHIANS 10:1-5

God's people in the Old Testament knew of nothing more solid, more permanent, or more secure than one of those great outcroppings of rock to which they and their forefathers had fled when the enemy pressed upon them. And so they often addressed God as their Rock, their place of refuge and strength in times of trouble.

God's people of the new covenant also cry unto a Lord who is their Rock, for as St. Paul tells the Corinthians, the spiritual Rock from which we drink is Christ. It is to Him that we flee for refuge when our enemies become too much for us; it is to Him that we go when we are thirsty for the water of life. It is on Him that God has built His church, God's castle, against which even the powers of hell itself can never prevail.

Christians are sometimes accused of being cowards or escapists because, when troubles come, they go running to God instead of standing like men and fighting their own battles. But it is not cowardice for troops to establish themselves on a mountainside where the enemy cannot reach them and where they have the surrounding countryside under observation and fire. We know the strength of the enemies that are massed against us—the principalities, the powers, the rulers of the darkness of this world—and we know that we cannot defeat them on their own ground. But up on the Rock—there our enemies cannot get at us, there we have the whole battlefield under our control, there we have living water to refresh us in the dust and heat of the battle.

When we cry to the Lord our Rock, therefore, it is not the whimper of a coward but the exultant shout of veteran combat troops that have discovered an impregnable base of operations. And we flee to the Rock, not to escape the battle but to strike at our enemies from the one point on the whole battlefield which they can never hope to occupy.

Trust God and Enjoy Life

1 Timothy 6:17

There seems to be a widespread notion that Christians are gloomy people who miss out on all of the fun of this world while they keep their hearts and eyes fixed on the world to come.

Now, it is true, of course, that Christians know they have here no abiding city. It is also true that they share, with the rest of mankind, the sorrows and sufferings and afflictions of a world that lies under the dominion of sin and death. And just because they know more about the reality of sin and death than other people do, Christians are likely to see more clearly than others the deep, underlying tragedy of life.

But the Christian also knows, as others do not, that he is living in a redeemed world and that the God who made and still governs this world is his gracious and loving heavenly Father. He knows that suffering does not come accidentally—and neither does joy. All things come from God, who has a purpose in sending them.

The good things that God sends are not, to the Christians, "lucky breaks" but gifts from his gracious Father, and they are to be received with joy and thanksgiving. The Christian who does not know how to enjoy the pleasures of family and friends, of food and drink, of nature and art, of work and play still has some growing up to do. He needs to remind Himself that this is the world God created and pronounced very good—and very good it still is despite all that sin has done to mar it.

Trust God and enjoy life—this is a good prescription for the Christian life, God's own prescription backed up by His promise that He will give us richly all things to enjoy.

The Bread of Life
JOHN 6:47-51

The Germans have a saying: "Man is what he eats." This may not be quite true physically, but it is certainly true spiritually. The man who feeds his heart and mind on smutty literature finds himself becoming more and more a creature of lust. The man who nourishes his soul on dreams of wealth and status and glory finds himself becoming more and more an unhappy victim of unsatisfied (and often unsatisfiable) ambitions.

The proper food for a man's soul is the Bread of Life, the Christ who is set before him in the written Word of God and in the Sacraments. He is the Bread which came down from heaven that a man might eat of it and not die. As the living Father sent Him into the world, so those who eat Him shall live eternally in Him and He in them. And those who will not eat Him must die, for there is no other food that can sustain the life of the spirit.

When our Lord told His countrymen these things, many of those who had followed Him up to that point turned their backs on Him. It all sounds too crude — doesn't it? — this eating flesh and drinking blood. Perhaps so. But there is much in the Christian religion that is not refined, not polite, not nice. Those who are well do not need a doctor, and those who are full do not need food. If the Bread of Life offends us, it is probably because we are not hungry enough to appreciate it. And if we are not hungry, it is probably because we have been gorging ourselves on the wrong food.

We were meant to live forever. God has given us the food to nourish our lives eternally. Come, then, Lord Jesus, be our Guest, and let this gift to us be blessed.

As Little Children . . .

Mark 10:13-16

When a number of parents brought their children to Jesus for His blessing, the disciples tried to shoo them away. After all, the Master was a busy man. Why should He be expected to take time out from His important work of teaching and healing to talk to a bunch of chattering, squirming small fry who might even tug around on His cloak and soil it with their dirty hands?

"But when Jesus saw it, He was much displeased and said unto them: 'Suffer the little children to come unto Me and forbid them not, for of such is the kingdom of God.' " With these few words He put the children at ease and the disciples in their place. To the children He revealed Himself as the gracious Lord who refuses no one who comes to Him. To the disciples He said in effect: "You still have a lot to learn about Me, and these children are the ones who can teach you."

But what could a little child teach a Peter or a James or a John? Jesus put it all into one word: humility. Except you humble yourselves and become as little children, you cannot enter the kingdom of God. There is no place in the Kingdom for anyone who thinks he can talk to God man to man. God is our Father—not our buddy or our pal. We do not come into His presence to slap Him on the back or to give Him instructions. We come to worship Him, to ask His forgiveness, and to receive His blessing.

A child knows that he is small, that he is weak, that he has much to learn. Adults are tempted to think they are strong and important and know it all. And so they have to be reminded over and over again that before God they are still little children. It is not a very flattering thought, but when we finally swallow our pride and accept ourselves for what we are, He gives us a greatness that we could never dare to hope for: He takes us up in His arms, puts His hand upon us, and blesses us.

God Is Able

JUDE 24-25

In this world the Christian is called to take up his cross and follow Jesus; to work before the night comes when no man can work; to wrestle with principalities and powers and the rulers of the darkness of this world; to fight the good fight of faith. The Christian who seeks to escape the hardships and perils of this calling finds soon enough that there is no escape except that of the turncoat who deserts to the enemy.

But it is not escapism for the Christian soldier to remind himself over and over again of the purpose of it all. Even our Lord endured the cross and despised its shame for the sake of the glory that was set before Him, and why should we who follow Him deny ourselves the comfort and the encouragement that sustained Him?

The promise is that the sufferings of this present time will be followed by glory and exceeding joy in the presence of God. The question of our worthiness does not arise. St. Francis of Assisi once said: "What a man is in the sight of God, that he is, and no more." This is true. But it is equally true that "what a man is in the sight of God, that he is, and no less." We who now fight the great unequal fight with sin, death, and our rebellious natures are destined for joy and peace, approval and honor in the courts of heaven—not because we have earned them but because we are brothers and sisters of Jesus Christ.

And because God has destined us for these joys, we know that they are already ours in a sense. He is able to keep us from falling. He is able to preserve us, even in the midst of perils, unto His heavenly kingdom. And so we fight and suffer and endure, not as men caught up in a hopeless situation but as conquerors who already have victory in their grasp and an invincible Captain at their side.

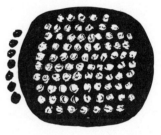

Burden Support
GALATIANS 6:1-10

Of all the great figures of the Bible the one most of us can understand best is Simon Peter. Peter was not what some nice, religious people would call a saint. He loved his Lord, and he tried to live up to what his Lord expected of him, but he had his own ideas about how far one could go with this religion business.

One day, after Peter had apparently been mulling over Jesus' insistence on forgiveness, he came up with what must have seemed to him the last word on the subject: "How often shall my brother sin against me and I forgive him? Until seven times?"

This was really quite a concession for a man like Peter to make. Judging from what we know of his hot, impetuous personality, we would say that it was not an easy thing for him to forgive at all. But if his Lord wanted him to forgive, he would do it—until seven times! Peter may well have expected Jesus to say: "Peter, that's wonderful. Congratulations! Now you are beginning to think and talk like a Christian." Instead, Jesus says: "I say not seven times, but seventy times seven."

Now, honestly, isn't this asking a bit too much? And this isn't the whole story. We are expected to be loving and patient and generous and kind—all day long, every day, all our lives. We are expected to bear other men's burdens, in addition to our own. We are expected to be holy! What does God think we are, angels?

No, God does not think we are angels. He knows how quickly we become weary in well-doing, and He stands ready to cover our weakness with His forgiveness. He doesn't leave it at that. But He is trying to make new persons of us, and He is not content with our making only a half-effort to overcome evil and do good.

Living and Walking in the Spirit

GALATIANS 5:16-24

It would be interesting to know who first came up with the ridiculous idea that Christians are calm, placid people with a perpetual smile on their faces and a song in their hearts. There is, it is true, a peace of God that surpasses all understanding and that sustains the Christian amid all the chances and changes of this life, but the essence of the Christian life is struggle, an inner war between flesh and spirit, which goes on from the moment of Baptism until the final great victory at the moment of death.

The fact that a person is a Christian does not mean that he is not tempted by the lusts of the flesh. Christians, too, have lustful desires, evil appetites, hot and undisciplined emotions. Christians know all too well what it is to be angry without good cause, to envy the good fortune of other men, to carry grudges, to get involved in useless quarrels. There are Christians who are still in the grip of superstition or of evil ambitions or of drink.

The Christian does not deal with these "works of the flesh" by pretending that they don't exist or by hoping that they will just disappear of their own accord. He crucifies the flesh with its affections and lusts—and this is a painful business. And in the place of these weeds of his old, sinful nature he cultivates the fruits of the Spirit—love, joy, peace, longsuffering, gentleness, goodness, 'faith, meekness, and temperance.

Living and walking in the Spirit is not, therefore, a leisurely stroll through some idyllic Eden, but a daily pilgrimage to the foot of the Cross. "They that are Christ's have crucified the flesh with the affections and lusts," and they walk in the Spirit on feet that bear the scars of nails.

In Everything Enriched
1 CORINTHIANS 1:4-9

Let's be honest about it. Most of us would like to be rich. We know that "you can't take it with you," but we know also that "it" is very pleasant to have while you are here.

God, who made all of the good things of the earth, has no quarrel with our desire to enjoy whatever is good. What troubles Him is that so often, in our pursuit of good things, we neglect or sacrifice the best. Money, friendship, love, a comfortable home, a good job—these are all good things and worth working for. But good as these things are, God has better things to offer us—the forgiveness of sins, fellowship with His Son, a part to play in the building of His church, everlasting life.

Very small children who are offered the choice between a bright, new penny and a wrinkled dollar bill are likely to choose the penny. Many of us who are no longer children continue to make this same childish choice. In so doing we refuse to let our Father enrich us. In our infatuation with the passing glory of the temporal, we reject the lasting glory of the eternal.

St. Paul thanked God that the Christians in Corinth had been enriched in "all utterance and in all knowledge." These are still the best gifts God can give to His children: to know God as their Father in Jesus Christ and to "utter" this knowledge in words and in behavior to those who have not yet heard this Good News. He who has these gifts and nothing else is rich, for he has treasures that he can take with him into eternity. He who has everything else but lacks these gifts is poor, both in this life and in eternity.

Sell, Give, and Follow
MATTHEW 19:16-22

"The young man had great possessions." No, that isn't quite right. Great possessions had the young man. He didn't own them; they owned him. And so, if he wanted to have eternal life, he had to rid himself of the tyrant that kept him tied to the fears and anxieties and frustrations of this world. "Sell that thou hast . . . give to the poor . . . follow Me."

"And the young man went away sorrowful." He knew the Law; he really believed he had kept it. But here in this decisive moment he was confronted with the demands of the First Commandment—"Thou shalt have no other gods before Me"—and he went away sorrowful. For he did have another god. And when the chips were down, it was this god, his possessions, that owned his heart and commanded his loyalty.

This was precisely what Jesus was trying to tell him. He had said it before in other words: "No man can serve two masters. . . . Ye cannot serve God and Mammon." God's claims are absolute. He will be everything or nothing to man. "He that loveth father or mother more than Me is not worthy of Me; and he that loveth son or daughter more than Me is not worthy of Me."

The rich young man was told to sell all that he had because his possessions had become his god. And he went away sorrowful, for he could not give up his god. Another man might have gone away sorrowful if he had been asked to give up his wife or his job or his political party or his hobby or his car.

What is it that I will not give up to follow Christ? That is my god. That is what I must be willing to give up to inherit eternal life.

Kingdom First

LUKE 12:22-31

The kingdom of God is God's rule in the hearts and lives of men. It was this kingdom that Jesus came to bring—and indeed He has brought it wherever His Spirit has turned men and women from the old self-centered way of life to that new life which is an imitation of Christ.

Those who seek this kingdom are intent, as was their Lord, upon working the works of God while it is day. They find purpose and meaning in life in feeding the hungry, clothing the naked, giving drink to the thirsty, visiting the sick and the imprisoned, doing good to all men. They are in the world not to be ministered unto but to minister and to give their lives as a sacrifice for many. They love their enemies, do good to those who hate them, and pray for those who mistreat and persecute them.

Being thus intent, they are also content; for in their slavery to God they win freedom from their old slavery to things. They no longer feel driven to keep up with the Joneses. They do not have to bolster their sense of self-importance by piling up money or honors or titles. They do not have to assert their own superiority by making other people feel inferior. All that they really need God stands ready to give them, pressed down and overflowing. And what they do not need they no longer feel compelled to long for and work for and struggle for.

Whenever we pray, "Thy kingdom come," we are praying that God would move farther and farther into our hearts, overthrowing all of the little idols that hold us in bondage and extending His rule and government over us. The prayer must be repeated daily, for the coming of the Kingdom is an ongoing process which is never completed in this life. But the greater its control over our hearts, the greater our joy and peace and contentment.

Good Tree, Good Fruit

MATTHEW 7:15-23

No one has to coax or beg an apple tree to bear apples. If it is a healthy tree, it will produce. And if it is not a healthy tree, no amount of coaxing or begging will bring out the apples.

So it is with people. We spend a great deal of time trying by threats or by coaxing to induce ourselves and one another to forsake sin and give ourselves to good works. But nothing much ever happens. We go on day after day repeating the old sins and making the same good resolutions that we have broken a thousand times. Some of us finally give up and resign ourselves to whatever punishment a just God may choose to inflict on us. Others of us keep trying and end up with ulcers or a heart attack or a bad case of jangled nerves.

In either case we pay a frightful price for refusing to let God be God in our lives. If we would worry less about doing good and concern ourselves more with being good, life would be both simpler and happier. For to be good, as God understands goodness, is simply to be forgiven — and this we already are if we will only believe it. This is why Jesus Christ came into the world and died on the cross and rose from the dead — to make us good and acceptable in the eyes of His Father. There is nothing we can add to what He has already done.

When His power works within us, we can "do what comes naturally" — naturally not to our old nature but to the new nature which He has created in us. Everything we do according to His power is good — not because of the nature of the work but because it is acceptable to God.

Make Us Faithful
1 CORINTHIANS 4:1-5

Does it make any real difference whether we believe in a Lord who "will come again in glory to judge both the quick and the dead"? Shouldn't we do the will of God just because it is His will and not because we hope for rewards or fear punishment?

God's threats are not idle threats. If we once understand what it is He threatens we will not take them lightly. We will fear them, as He intends us to do. By the same token, His promised rewards are real and desirable rewards, and since He has promised them, we have every right to encourage ourselves and one another by looking forward to them in joyful anticipation.

The life we live on this earth is the life of a steward, of a trustee. The Master who has entrusted His wealth to us will come again, and when He comes He will require an accounting. We shall be brought into judgment.

Knowing this, we have every reason to take our stewardship seriously. God's grace is free, but it is not cheap. The same God who said, "By grace are ye saved through faith," said also, "Work out your own salvation with fear and trembling" and "be fruitful in every good work." He has not forgiven us so that we may waste His gifts on riotous living or squander His wealth on the gratification of our lusts. He has forgiven us so that "we may be His own, and live under Him in His kingdom, and serve Him in everlasting righteousness, innocence, and blessedness."

The man who thinks that he can take all that God has to offer and give nothing of himself in return will find out soon enough that not everyone who says, "Lord! Lord!" will enter into the kingdom of heaven. We pray today that God would make us faithful stewards, because only those who by His power and grace do the will of the Father have any place in His kingdom.

Religion of Little Things
JAMES 1:22-27

When Naaman the leper came to the prophet Elisha seeking a cure for his leprosy, he was mightily offended when Elisha told him to go and dip himself seven times in the muddy little Jordan. Here was this great general, ready to pay any price, prepared to undergo any amount of suffering, and the prophet sends him off to do something that any penniless child could do. What kind of God was this God of Elisha's? Hadn't He ever heard of the great Naaman?

There is some of Naaman in all of us. Let God tell us to make a pilgrimage to the Holy Land, and we will borrow the money to do it. Let Him tell us to climb six flights of marble steps on our knees, and we will do it not once but twice. But let Him tell us to give a helping hand to a widow or an orphan, and we go off in a huff. What is religious about a simple act that anybody can do? Can't God think of some project big enough to allow us to show our stuff?

God operates with a different scale of values than we do. His Son illustrates the meaning of the word "Master" by washing His disciples' feet. He warns us of a day when we will be judged not on the basis of how many millions we have given to charity or how many offices we held in the church but how we treated the hungry and the thirsty and the naked and the sick and the imprisoned.

What we call the little things are the very things that God really asks of us. And so often what we call the big things are merely a lot of window-dressing.

We Are What We Are by Grace
1 CORINTHIANS 15:1-10

What does it mean to be humble?

Does it mean that we must deny the gifts and abilities that God has given us? Does it mean that we must pretend that we are stupid if we actually are intelligent, ugly if we actually happen to be beautiful, or poor if God has blessed us with wealth?

St. Paul was a truly humble man. But he sounds anything but humble when he says that he labored more abundantly than all the rest of the apostles. What he said happened to be true, and one thing we can learn from him is that humility does not require us to become liars. What it really requires is that we be perfectly honest with ourselves.

The essence of true Christian humility is the recognition that God has given us whatever abilities, characteristics, and achievements we have, as tools to be used in the doing of a job, not as ornaments to be displayed for our own amusement or for impressing other people. We are ambassadors for Christ, and every gift that God has given us is intended to help us do the great job of representing Him in the world.

Let a man really try to use his talents responsibly and effectively in his Lord's service, and he will learn soon enough that "unless God gives both thought and deed, the utmost pains can ne'er succeed, and vain must be man's might." Then he will be truly humble, for he will know that it is finally only the grace of God in him that makes him what he is and enables him to accomplish whatever he does accomplish. And knowing that, he will be content to be what God has made him, whether great or small.

The Spirit Rests
1 CORINTHIANS 12:1-11

The early church, like the church in our own day, had to contend with people in its own membership who thought that certain kinds of Christian service were, in themselves, more "religious," more "holy" than others. The man who was able to work miracles was tempted to suppose that he stood at least a little higher on the scale than did the man who could merely speak in tongues. And the man who could speak in tongues was tempted to look down on the man who was just an "ordinary" preacher.

We are suspicious nowadays of miracle-workers and men who claim to be able to speak in tongues. But many of us consider the holy ministry a more "religious" calling than the teaching ministry, and probably most of us see nothing at all "holy" or "religious" in the ordinary weekday labors of lay people. Indeed, many laymen seem to be troubled by the feeling that their regular jobs have no real meaning and that if they were really first-rate Christians they would give up whatever they are doing and enter a seminary.

There are, of course, those who are called late in life to professional service in the church. But not every Christian would make a good preacher or a good theologian or a good organist. The church also needs good janitors, good trustees, good artists and painters, good journalists, good laymen who will live and speak the Gospel of Christ in the ordinary routines of their jobs and professions.

What makes any Christian's work holy or religious is not the nature of the work itself but the fact that the Spirit of God rests upon him as he does the work. And that Spirit rests upon all of us, whatever our callings, who are children of God by faith in Jesus Christ.

Our Sufficiency Is of God

2 Corinthians 3:4-11

Most of us feel vaguely uncomfortable from time to time about witnessing to our faith. We know that we ought to be doing it—but we hesitate to try it for fear of doing it badly.

There is a certain decent humility in this hesitation to thrust ourselves into a work which, at its best, claimed the full time and the great talents of such giants as the prophets, the apostles, the reformers, the inspired teachers and preachers of the church. "Shoemaker, stick to your last" is pretty sound advice, and most of us know that we were never cut out to be preachers or evangelists.

But every Christian is called to be a "minister of the new testament," a "little apostle." We cannot help speaking the things that we have seen and heard. To keep them bottled up inside us for fear of speaking poorly, or perhaps even wrongly, is to forget who we are—God's people, ministers of Jesus Christ, instruments of the Holy Spirit.

No man, not even a Paul or an Isaiah or a Luther, has it in his power to create faith by the brilliance or eloquence of his own witness. It was Paul himself who said, "Our sufficiency [as able ministers of the new testament] is of God." If this was true of the greatest of the apostles, it must be doubly and triply true of us. Our sufficiency, too, is of God. That is to say, God can use our poor, simple, stammering tongues for the very same purpose that He used Paul's learning and persuasiveness, as the means through which the Holy Spirit transmits "the power of God unto salvation, through faith in Christ Jesus."

Crown of Thorns
MATTHEW 27:27-31

In His lifetime Jesus was always being mistaken for the wrong kind of king. Herod tried to kill Him because he misunderstood what the Wise Men meant when they called Him "the king of the Jews." Satan thought he could bargain with Him, as he had bargained with many another king, for a throne that would cost nothing but a denial of His Father. The people of Israel saw all the qualities of kingship in Him when He fed a multitude with five barley loaves and two small fishes. And Pilate, writing better than he knew, wrote a title and put it on His cross: JESUS OF NAZARETH THE KING OF THE JEWS.

It remained for a detachment of pagan soldiers to crown Him with the only crown He was willing to accept. They platted a crown of thorns and put it on His head — and He did not refuse it. For this was the crown which His Father had prepared for Him, and by it He would assert His lordship over sin, death, and hell.

Men still mistake Jesus for the wrong kind of king. They try to make Him the symbol of some race or nation or sect. They try to build His kingdom with power and the sword. They try to make Him a mere bread-giver. They try to depict Him as a false king who cannot hold His own against the men of steel and blood who "really run things" on this earth.

But today, as in His earthly lifetime, the Lord Jesus refuses every crown except the crown of thorns—the symbol of His victory, the seal of our liberation. By this crown we recognize our rightful King—the King who came not as a despot to enslave us but as a liberator to set us free.

Well Pleased

MATTHEW 17:1-9

"Blessed are they that have not seen and yet have believed."

"We walk by faith, not by sight" (2 Cor. 5:7). If we make our faith in Jesus Christ dependent on signs and wonders—even such a mighty sign as the Transfiguration—we are no better than the Pharisees who demanded a sign from the Lord and were told, "An evil and adulterous generation seeketh after a sign; and there shall no sign be given to it but the sign of the prophet Jonas."

But God, who always gives His people more than they have any right to ask or think, has given us in the New Testament eyewitness accounts of events so extraordinary in the life of our Lord that only the stubbornest unbelief can refuse to accept them as signs that He was someone unique among men. And unless one is prepared to say that these eyewitnesses were blind, deaf, and dumb—and liars on top of it all—he has little choice but to accept their testimony as a factual account of what they saw and heard.

Faith is more, though, than accepting a Scriptural account as true. The devils believe that Jesus Christ was transfigured on the holy mount—and tremble. I believe that He who is fairer than the children of men is truly what the Father declared Him to be: His beloved Son, in whom He is well pleased. And since by my baptism I have been made one with Him, I dare to believe that the Father is also well pleased with me. Believing this, I look forward with full confidence to the day when I myself shall see the Son in His glory sitting at the right hand of God—not on a mountaintop from which I must return to the cares and troubles of this world but in the everlasting courts of heaven.

All

LUKE 10:23-37

The lawyer was right. If a man would inherit eternal life, he need only keep the law of God. "This do," Jesus says, "and thou shalt live."

But the trick is in the doing. It isn't too hard to love God with one's heart and mind and soul and strength. Any man can do that now and then and more or less. The trouble lies with that little word *all*. How can anyone possibly love God with all his heart and all his soul and all his strength and all his mind?

And that isn't all. "Thou shalt love thy neighbor as thyself." A man might be able to delude himself into thinking that he has done his full duty to God, whom he has never seen. But no one in his right mind could imagine that he has ever loved any other human being as he loves himself. We know all too well how we have treated the people around us—our parents, our husband or wife, our children, our boss, our employees, the man next door, the woman down the street.

So when our Lord says, "This do and thou shalt live," He is really saying, "You can't be saved by the Law." The Law was never intended to save men. It was intended to drive them to a recognition of their desperate need for God's mercy and forgiveness.

This does not mean that the Law does not have to be obeyed. It is God's law, and it is backed up by His Word: "Cursed be he that confirmeth not all the words of this Law to do them." The hard truth which the Law itself teaches us is that we cannot obey it — and therefore we must look elsewhere for eternal life, to the Christ who took our curse upon Himself and thus destroyed the Law's power to condemn us.

Down a Notch
LUKE 18:9-14

Even the decent non-Christian does not have much use for the man who "toots his own horn." That we are all the victims of false pride does not mean that we admire it in others. Actually, most of us get a kind of pleasure out of seeing a proud man "taken down a notch."

Unfortunately, it is always easier to see the mote of pride in another man's eye than to recognize the beam of pride in our own eye. What we call pride or arrogance or self-exaltation in another man we call self-confidence or self-respect in ourselves. Sometimes, indeed, we even call it humility. Thus we may brag about our abilities or our children or our country or our church all we like, so long as we remember to tack on a "Thank God" or a "To God alone be the glory."

But there is no point to deceiving ourselves. "Everyone that exalteth himself shall be abased." The braggart who boasts that he can lick any man in the house will eventually get his comeuppance — but so will the good church member who, like the Pharisee in the parable, thanks God that he is not as other men are.

It is not that God enjoys beating us down and making us feel small. He simply wants us to be honest with Him and with ourselves. We are small and foolish and sick and sinful — and it is only at the point where we see ourselves for what we really are that He can begin to make us great and wise and healthy and clean. False pride tells God: "I don't need You." False humility tells God: "I'm such a mess that even You can't make anything of me." Real humility tells God: "Just as I am I come to You to be made into what You want me to be."

The Angry Jesus
LUKE 19:41-48

It is almost impossible for flesh and blood to obey St. Paul's command: "Be ye angry, and sin not." We can become angry all right, but what makes us angry is almost always some personal slight or some frustration of our own wills. Our anger is therefore seldom the "righteous indignation" to which St. Paul exhorts us and which our Lord displayed in His cleansing of the temple.

But even though it may be beyond our capabilities, there is such a thing as righteous indignation. When God's honor is besmirched, when His Gospel is perverted or denied, when His children are mistreated, when some idol demands the fear and love which only God has the right to demand, the Christian can and should become angry. And his anger should spur him to action to correct the wrong.

The Christ of the Gospels is not merely a "gentle Jesus, meek and mild." He is also the angry Jesus who lashed out against the scribes and Pharisees, who pronounced woe upon the theologians of His day, who took a whip and drove the money changers out of the temple. He could show boundless kindness and love to those who hated Him, even to those who betrayed and crucified Him. But He reacted with cold fury to those who dishonored His Father.

Even His anger, though, was intended to bring men to repentance. He broke up the "den of thieves" so that His Father's house could again be what it was intended to be—a house of prayer—also for those thieves. This is always the purpose of God's wrath, to lash men to repentance. This must be our purpose also if our anger is to be, in any real sense of the word, righteous indignation.

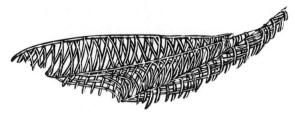

Strong Nets
LUKE 5:1-11

Fishing was serious business for the disciples of our Lord. They made their living as fishermen, and a bad catch—or no catch at all—put quite a hole into their family budgets.

And since fishing was serious business for these hardworking men, the Lord who loved them also took it seriously. He knew they had to eat and pay taxes and buy clothing and keep their houses in repair. So when He saw them in trouble, He did something about it. He told them where to let down their net, and then He sent a multitude of fishes to fill it.

"And their net brake." This is one of the ironies of the Christian life. We are never equipped to receive all that God wants to give us. The net is not strong enough to hold the multitude of fishes which He sends us, the cup runs over because it is not large enough to hold the goodness and mercy which He pours into it, the heart cannot contain the love and kindness and peace with which He wants to fill it.

We have to be careful, therefore, when we pray. The real question is not how much God is willing to give—He is willing to give exceeding abundantly above all that we ask or think — but how much we are able to receive. We had better not go fishing in the deep waters of God's generosity unless we have nets strong enough to hold the catch. We had better not pray at all than ask for more than our hearts or hands or minds can hold.

Indeed, our first prayer should not be for fishes or wine or even love, but for a net strong enough to hold the catch, for a cup large enough to hold the wine, for a heart open far enough to receive His love. This is the kind of prayer to which our Lord urges us when He says: "Seek ye first the kingdom of God and His righteousness." Then — and only then — can and will "all these things be added unto you."

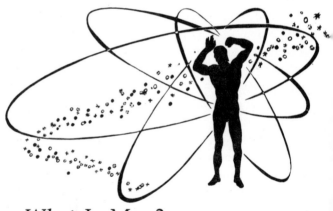

What Is Man?

Luke 15:1-10

One answer is that he is a rather short-lived creature, one of more than three billion similar creatures crawling over the surface of a small planet in one of the many solar systems of one of the numberless galaxies that make up the universe. He lives, he eats, he reproduces, he dies, and neither his living nor his dying makes any real difference to anyone except himself and perhaps the half dozen or so friends and relatives who loved him.

But the God who set the galaxies in motion and who holds the whole universe in His hand like some mechanical toy has quite another answer to the question. He says—and we can believe it only because He says it—that each of us is important enough in the grand scheme of things that we can break His heart or send Him into transports of joy. Less than specks of dust though we may be in the vastness of the universe, we were created to outlive it. Short-lived as we are, we shall see the day when our sun is only a memory and our galaxy a half-forgotten legend.

This sounds presumptuous. It sounds like the big talk of little children who still have to learn how small and insignificant they really are. But it is not man's talk; it is God's talk. "Rejoice with Me!" Why? Because He has created a new galaxy? Because He has exploded another sun? Because He has set a new nebula spinning? No—"for I have found My sheep which was lost—My little, foolish sheep which doesn't matter much to anybody else but matters a great deal to Me."

All this raises a question we ought to ask ourselves from time to time: If every one of His sheep means so much to God, shouldn't we mean much more than we do to one another?

Our Battle in Gethsemane

MATTHEW 26:36-46

The disciples followed Jesus — and He led them to Gethsemane.

This was not at all the destination they had been dreaming of those three years they followed Him up and down the Holy Land. Their eyes had been fixed on Jerusalem and the throne they expected their Lord to claim for Himself as the rightful ruler of Israel. They had even quarreled among themselves as to who would sit where in the throne room.

But He led them to Gethsemane.

No wonder they slept. What was there to see or do in Gethsemane? What did this midnight visit to a garden have to do with the main business of the Son of David? True, Jesus had told them that this would be a fateful night, that they would be put to the test and would fail Him. But they had not understood Him. How could they when even the priests and theologians were waiting for a king who would restore the kingdom to Israel?

So, while they slept, they missed the first skirmish in the King's great battle to recover His throne. History was being made, and they slept right through it. They came with Jesus to Gethsemane, but they might as well have stayed in Jerusalem.

Jesus brings us day by day and year by year to Gethsemane. Does it mean any more to us than it did to the Eleven? What do we see in the Garden—the reality of God Himself doing battle with the powers of darkness, or drowsy visions of reserved seats at His right hand? "He that is not with Me is against Me," our Lord says. The heart that still lingers among the glories of Jerusalem while the Son of God does lonely battle in Gethsemane is not with Him.

"Watch, therefore, and pray that ye enter not into temptation!"

Our Eternal Hope
1 Corinthians 15:55-58

It would be the rankest ingratitude to despise the countless good things that God gives us in this life—husband or wife, children, food, clothing, shelter, friends, the beauty of nature, the achievements of men, and whatever else makes our life good and pleasurable.

But even God's best blessings would be bittersweet indeed if in one sudden moment our lives could be snuffed out forever. We were not made for death but for life, and life would be a cruel joke if it were nothing more than the prelude to death and destruction and decay.

The hope that Christian people have in the resurrection of the body and the life everlasting is not a self-seeking hope of reward; Christian people know that they have deserved no reward. Rather it is hope in the God who created life and who will not have His good and gracious purposes frustrated. And this is no sentimental hope; it is a certain hope anchored in the historical fact that God Himself, in the person of Jesus Christ, endured death so that by His rising from the dead He might demonstrate His mastery over death and the grave.

It was the good news of this hope that the first Christian missionaries carried out into a world that was without hope and without God. Some believed and for the sake of this hope endured persecution and death. Many rejected it, preferring a life of hopelessness to this "nonsense" about a resurrection from the dead. This is still the good news which God's people have to bring to the world. Some will accept, many will reject. Praise God, our confidence in this hope does not rest in man's acceptance or rejection of it but in the promise of the risen Christ: "Because I live, ye too shall live."

One God and Father of All

EPHESIANS 4:1-6

At last count, there were something like 250 different religious denominations in the United States. But there is only one church. More than 112 million Americans are listed as members of some Christian denomination. But there is only one body. New sects spring up every day. But if they are Christian at all, they confess, in the words of the Nicene Creed, that the church is one, holy, Christian, and apostolic.

This oneness in the church is the same kind of oneness that exists in a family where all of the children have the same father. Children may quarrel among themselves, but they cannot escape the fact of their brotherhood. Nor, if their father is a good father, can they expect him to show partiality among his children. The prodigal son is as dear to his father as is the son who never left home.

Since this is so, the church cannot and will not allow the hatreds, the fears, the suspicions, and the prejudices which divide man from man to break that bond of peace which unites her children in the household of God. In Christ there is no East or West, no male or female, no Jew or Greek, no white man or Negro or Oriental, no upper class or middle class or lower class, no Catholic or Protestant. The one, holy, Christian, and apostolic church is a brotherhood of sinners who have been redeemed, restored, and forgiven — nothing more and nothing less.

From this it follows that no man can truly call God his Father unless he is willing to call every one of God's children his brother. And no church can be truly the house of God unless its doors are open to every child of God who may wish to meet his Father there.

Members Together in Christ

Ephesians 4:22-28

The meaning of the word "member" has changed in the course of time. Its most usual meaning used to be "an organ of the body, especially a limb." Today it usually means a person who belongs to some organization.

The Bible always uses the word "member" in its old sense. We are members together in Christ in the same way that our hands and feet are members of our bodies. A broken leg puts the whole body out of commission. Gangrene in an arm would threaten the whole body.

When St. Paul warns the Christians at Ephesus against lying and stealing and unjust anger, he does not say, "For these are violations of the Ten Commandments" — although they certainly are that. No, he appeals to a still higher law — the law of Christian love — and says, "You must not lie to one another or steal from one another or be unjustly angry with one another, because such behavior is like an infection in the body of Christ, of which you are all members."

There are, in other words, no purely personal or private sins, any more than there are injuries or illnesses which affect only the arm or the leg. Health is a condition of the whole body, and illness is a condition of the whole body. So also the conduct of the individual Christian affects the health of the whole body of Christ.

It is easy to point out flaws and faults in the church. It is much harder to face up to the question: "Am I perhaps one of the sources from which this infection has been seeping through the body?" If I am—and I most certainly am—then let the healing process begin with me, with my cleansing in the blood of Jesus Christ.

Acceptance
JOHN 4:40-42

It is a comforting thing to know that Jesus spent two days with Samaritans. As a good Jew, He should not even have spoken to them, much less have entered their homes. For the Samaritans had perverted the worship of the true God, had separated themselves from the worship of His temple in Jerusalem, and had adopted many of the ideas and beliefs of the surrounding heathen world. Association with a Samaritan was therefore a defilement to a Jew, and many Jews who made the journey between Galilee and Jerusalem went miles out of their way to avoid crossing "accursed Samaria."

But Jesus spent two days with these people, two days in which He must have shared in the whole round of their defiled and defiling lives. While He was with them, He told them who He was and why He had come into the world. And many believed in Him. Here, among the bitterest enemies of His chosen people, He made His first disciples outside the house of Israel.

Nowhere better than in Samaria could Jesus have demonstrated His willingness to accept "whosoever cometh to Me." If He could accept Samaritans, He could accept anyone—even us. More than that, if He could accept Samaritans, He stands ready to accept those whom we are so very unwilling to accept—people whom we despise because of their race or their language or their politics or their bad reputation in the community.

If we follow in the footsteps of this Jesus, He will lead us through the Samarias of our world and bring us into contact with all sorts of people whom we would rather avoid. But He will also give us the grace to accept them even as He has accepted us. This is what the Scriptures mean when they call His ministry and ours a ministry of reconciliation—a ministry through which men are reconciled to God through the death and resurrection of Jesus Christ and to one another through their adoption as sons of the same Father.

Sunrise on Good and Evil

MATTHEW 5:43-48

Life is not so very complicated a business if one uses a little common sense. There are a few people in the world who are so likable that one can't help loving them, and so one does; and the best thing about it is that usually the love is returned—which makes things pleasant all around. Then there are a few people who are just plain no good; the best way to handle them is to give them a good dose of their own medicine. And in between are those millions of people who don't count at all; neither friends nor enemies, they can be completely ignored.

The only trouble with this common-sensical way of dealing with people is that God won't allow it. "Love your enemies," He says. "Do good unto all men." What kind of talk is this? Does God expect the impossible of us?

Yes and no. Nothing is impossible if it has been done—and God does love His enemies. He makes His sun to rise on the evil and on the good; He made His Son a sacrifice for all men. So God is not asking anything more of us than He has already done for us. But, of course, we are not gods; we do not even have it in us to be very good imitators of God. The command to love our enemies is therefore an impossible demand.

Nevertheless, it is God's command, and we are held to obey it. God really does expect us to make the sun of our love and kindness and generosity to rise without partiality upon those we like and those we dislike. Our daily failure to do so should be a daily reminder of our great need for His forgiveness. The daily renewal of the command to love should be a daily reminder of our great need for His grace, which alone can give us the power to love. And each day's rising sun should be new testimony to that perfect love which, working in us, can transfigure us and make us shine with the reflected light of the loving God.

Pentecost Miracles Today

ACTS 2:1-13

Nothing like it had ever happened before. Nothing like it is likely ever to happen again.

But Pentecost is a miracle which, in a less dramatic way, the Spirit of God performs every day. For while any man can learn another language if he is willing to give sufficient time and effort to it, no man can call Jesus Lord but by the Holy Ghost. Therefore every time we call Jesus Lord we speak a language which is not native to us. We speak, in sober fact, as the Spirit gives us utterance.

And when we speak thus, chances are that we will get the same reaction that Peter and the apostles got from many in the crowd on that first Pentecost. "You're full of new wine," "You're crazy," "I don't dig you," "What kind of preacher talk is that?"—these are all ways of expressing the same reaction, a reaction of unbelief and sometimes hostility to the Gospel. And this need not surprise us, for the Gospel really is foolishness to those who do not believe.

But not everyone will mock us as madmen or drunks. Through the Word spoken by His people God adds to the church those who should be saved. There is a power in the Gospel which gives a kind of eloquence even to our fumbling and stumbling speech—not perhaps the eloquence of a Peter or a Paul but the simple eloquence of a child describing his father, of a shipwrecked sailor telling how he was rescued.

Pentecost was a miracle. But wherever the Holy Spirit is present in the Word, miracles happen. For faith itself is a great miracle, and every Christian is a living testimony to the miraculous working of the Holy Spirit.

God Is Faithful
1 CORINTHIANS 10:6-13

An English nobleman whose garden party was spoiled by an unexpected shower is supposed to have shaken his fist at the sky and exclaimed, "How like You, God!"

We would never do such a foolish and blasphemous thing, of course. We know that God is not a killjoy who goes about spoiling garden parties and generally taking all the fun out of life. And yet we don't like to talk about our good fortune without knocking on wood, and we cross our fingers when we make plans for the future.

The fact of the matter is that many of us, much of the time, unconsciously picture God as a kind of cruel practical joker who sits up in heaven devising some new kind of unpleasant surprise to drop on us when we least expect it. If we happen to have a string of "good luck," we suspect that He is just building us up for an awful letdown. If things are not going so well, we are sure that He is just trying to see how much we can take.

What we are actually doing when we picture God thus is re-creating Him in our own image. It would be just like us to play such practical jokes if we were God. It would be just like us to "really pour it on" some poor unfortunate who is already bearing about as much as he can bear. After all, we do it every day.

But God is not a man, certainly not a sinful man. He does indeed test His children, sometimes with unexpected misfortunes, but only because they need it. He does lay burdens upon His children, but only so that they may see that He is Himself helping them to bear them. In everything He does He is faithful, faithful to His own loving nature and to His vows of love to us.

Children and Heirs of God

ROMANS 8:12-17

If the President of the United States should choose to adopt the infant son of Public Enemy Number One, we would be surprised and, perhaps, a bit shocked. But we would be even more surprised and shocked if, having adopted the child, the President should then leave him in the care of his natural father and refuse to let him into the White House. We expect the parents of adopted children to treat them the same way they treat their own flesh and blood, and our moral sense is outraged if they do not. Our laws give adopted children the same inheritance rights as natural children, and our courts will insist that these rights be respected.

We are by nature the children of Public Enemy Number One. But we have been adopted by a Father far greater than the President of the United States. Perhaps it is the tremendous contrast between our natural father and our adoptive Father that makes it so difficult for us to believe that it all really happened. Do we really belong to the Royal Family or are we, perhaps, presuming too much? Can we always be sure that the palace is our home, or must we fear that someday we may be turned away and sent back to the miserable hovel that was once our home?

Well, is God less moral, less honorable than the President of the United States? Would we expect God to behave in a way that would outrage us if a man behaved so? Is there anything in our experience that teaches us that we must take God's own word and promise with a grain of salt?

God calls us His children and heirs. If we are not, He is a liar. If we are, why do we doubt His love, avoid His company, and fear His rejection?

Gifts, Not Wages
ROMANS 6:19-23

Sin is a good master in one respect. It pays its servants in full and on time. Sin is a good master also in another respect. It pays precisely what it has promised to pay. The sinner, therefore, who is forever demanding his "just deserts," who is forever insisting on what he is "entitled to," need not worry. He will get it, full measure and on time. He will die.

God, on the other hand, does not deal with us as a master but as a father. He does not dole out wages to us, and it is a good thing that He doesn't. For if He paid us what we have earned, we would receive a double death—once as the faithful servants of sin and a second time as the unfaithful servants of God.

Our hope, therefore, lies not in getting our "just deserts" but in receiving those free gifts which God gives to His children simply because He is their Father and because there is no limit to His generosity. All of these good gifts—forgiveness, peace, joy, faith, the ability to please Him—come wrapped up in one package which the New Testament labels "eternal life."

This life is eternal in two senses. It is a life that has no ending and will, therefore, survive even physical death. But it is also a life which here and now shares in God's eternal existence and therefore exhibits many of the qualities of God's own life. "The gift of God is eternal life," St. Paul says. Those who blaspheme Christianity as a "pie in the sky" religion had better get Christian teaching straight before they start condemning it.

This eternal life we have today and tomorrow and forever in Jesus Christ our Lord. It is His to give because by conquering death He became the Lord and Giver of life.

The Reach of Love
1 JOHN 3:13-18

So often when the Scriptures speak of love, they speak in the same breath of dying. Our Lord says, "Greater love hath no man than this, that he lay down his life for his friends." St. John says, "Hereby perceive we the love of

God, because He laid down His life for us; and we ought to lay down our lives for the brethren." (1 John 3:16)

Love is not sentimentality. It is not even just a kindly emotion. It is an act of sacrifice. Love gives and keeps on giving—even, if necessary, unto death.

Christian love, which is really God's love shining through His people, extends not only to friends and relatives, who "deserve" it, but to all men, even our enemies. The Christian cannot refuse to love anyone whom God has loved—and "God so loved the world."

Christian love reaches out with special warmth to "the brethren," to fellow believers. They are living reminders of God's eternal sacrifice, the same sacrifice by which we have been ransomed from sin and despair and death and given an inheritance among the saints in light.

Most of us will probably never be called upon to face death on the cross or at the stake or in the arena for our brethren. All of us, though, if we take love seriously, will learn that it means dying a little day by day—dying to selfishness, to resentment, to our own likes and dislikes, to that "I'll get even with you" attitude, to everything in us that insists on self-satisfaction at the expense of our brother's needs.

"May we, gracious Lord, ever be reminded of Thy eternal sacrifice, so that by its power we may lay down our lives for our brethren."

The Pulse and the Heartbeat

1 PETER 3:8-15

At first glance the Scriptures seem to contradict themselves when they speak about righteousness. St. Paul, for instance, speaks of a righteousness which is by faith and which has nothing to do with good works. St. Peter speaks of righteousness in terms of not rendering evil for evil, refraining our tongues from evil and our lips from speaking guile, turning away from evil and doing good, seeking peace and pursuing it.

So who is right—St. Peter or St. Paul? Are we saved by faith or by works or by a combination of faith and works?

Perhaps the question can be put in more understandable terms. How do we know that a man is alive? Is it because we can feel his pulse, or is it because we can put our ear to his chest and hear his heartbeat, or is it a combination of the two? Certainly the pulse is nothing more than evidence that the heart is beating. When the heart is functioning, there is a pulse. The absence of a pulse is pretty good evidence that the heart has stopped beating.

So also works and faith go together. Where there is faith, there are good works. Where good works are lacking, there is pretty good evidence that there is no faith.

But we must go one step further. The heartbeat itself is not the cause of life, but the means by which God preserves life. In the same way, our faith is not the reason why we are righteous before God, but the hand with which we receive forgiveness and every other good gift. Our spiritual life, like our physical life, is finally God's free gift.

We are saved by grace, the same grace that creates and preserves faith and that enables us to do those works which are pleasing to God. Faith and works, like heartbeat and pulse, go together because both are products of the same gracious work of God.

Lord, Help Us to Pray
LUKE 11:1-4

Prayer should come naturally to man. There is God — merciful and gracious, long-suffering, and worthy to be had in reverence by all the children of men. And there is man — dependent on God for every good and perfect gift and endowed with heart and mind and tongue to bring both his praises and his petitions to the heavenly throne.

But the disciples spoke for all of us when they asked our Lord to teach them how to pray; for between man and God stands the awful barrier of sin, which makes it impossible for us to pray as we ought. Until that barrier is broken down, it is simply out of the question for us to address the

Holy One as "Our Father." To do so would be a little too much like doing what Judas did when he betrayed the Son of Man with a kiss.

The disciples, who still had so much to learn about the person and work of their Master, probably did not fully understand what they were asking when they asked Him to help them to pray. But at least they asked for help from the right source, for their Master was not only able to teach them the right words; He was also able to break down the barrier which prevented men's prayers from reaching the Throne of Grace. He helped them and us to pray, by reconciling us to the Father by His life of blameless obedience and by His death on the cross.

We still pray the prayer He taught His disciples, but we are not limited to this one prayer. Every longing of our heart, every spoken or unspoken thought that focuses on God as the source of our help or hope or joy is a prayer, acceptable to God—for Jesus' sake.

Cure for Blindness
LUKE 18:31-43

The blind man who begged our Lord for the restoration of his sight had one great advantage over most of us; he knew he was blind.

We blunder our way through life proudly confident that our darkness is light and that the imaginings of our own hearts and minds are visions of reality. And so, when we read something like St. Paul's magnificent assertion of the power and permanence of love, we marvel at the beauty of the words and secretly wonder whether Paul was not letting himself be carried away a bit. After all, love doesn't seem to be all that powerful, and surely not all that permanent, in the "real" world.

Even our prayers seem sometimes to be nothing more than arrows shot into the unknown, for we cannot see the God whom we address, and it is not always obvious that He is our Rock and our Fortress, the God who does wonders for His people. Often enough, when we look toward heaven, we see nothing—nothing at all, and we are strongly tempted to listen to those who tell us that we see nothing because actually there is nothing there.

We need even more than blind Bartimaeus to pray therefore, "Lord, that I may receive my sight." For the blindness which afflicts us is not a mere defect in our eyes but a sickness in our souls. And for this sickness there is no cure except the hand of the Son of God laid upon us in mercy and in healing. But "they that are whole need not a physician." If we would be healed, we must admit we are blind and must ask Him as humbly and confidently as Bartimaeus did, "Lord, that I may receive my sight."

I Say, Arise

LUKE 7:11-17

If Jesus Christ had done all of the other mighty works recorded in the New Testament but had never demonstrated His power over death, we would have to wonder whether He was really all that He claimed to be. The bondage under which every one of us lives is the fear of death. We dread it not only because everything in us cries out against the threat of extinction but also because we know that death is not the natural destiny of man, that it is God's punishment for man's sin. It is this cause-and-effect relationship between sin and death that gives death its sting.

Any man, therefore, who claimed to be our savior from sin would have to be taken with a grain of salt unless he could remit the penalty of sin, which is death. And he would have to be able to do this in his own name and by his authority, for only the one who has been sinned against has any right to remit the penalty.

All this Jesus did when He told the young man of Nain, "I say unto thee, Arise!" Prophets and apostles, on those rare occasions when they raised the dead, did so in the name of God. But this Man says, "I say unto thee, Arise!" Only a fool or a madman or God Himself would dare to say such a thing in such surroundings, with a grieving mother looking on and a host of mourners ready to turn on Him if He failed.

Fools and madmen do not raise the dead. But the Son of Man, who has power on earth to forgive sins, has also the power to undo the consequences of sin, that is, to raise the dead. This power, after His resurrection, He gave to the church, the fellowship of the forgiven. And possessing this power, the church can confidently assure the bereaved and the sorrowing that their blessed dead, who died in His forgiveness, will hear the same voice that the young man of Nain once heard: "I say unto thee, Arise!"

Caesar and God

MATTHEW 22:15-22

If a man renders unto God, "of whom and through whom are all things," the things that belong to God, what is left for Caesar?

The answer is that the things which are Caesar's are those things which God Himself has given to Caesar—the power to punish evildoers, the right to collect taxes, the duty to maintain peace and order in the temporal affairs of men. In the discharge of these powers, rights, and duties Caesar acts as God's own minister, and those who resist him will, St. Paul says, "receive unto themselves damnation."

But there are many powers, rights, and duties which God has not delegated to Caesar. Some of these He has delegated to other ministers — especially the family and the church. Others He has reserved for Himself. When a German Caesar sets out to destroy a whole people or when a Russian Caesar attempts to liquidate religion, the Christian citizen must render unto God the things that are God's, even though it means resisting Caesar.

One of the blessings we have enjoyed is the willingness of our "Caesars" to let God be God. Like all blessings, it is one to which we become quickly accustomed. We therefore need to remind ourselves that it is a very great blessing indeed — one which very few people have ever enjoyed — and that it deserves not only the gratitude of our hearts but the labors of our hands and minds.

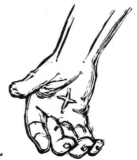

Greet the Savior, Face the Judge

1 PETER 4:7-11

It is now almost 2,000 years since our Lord ascended into heaven. For a few years after His ascension His disciples lived with the words of the two men in white apparel ringing in their ears: "This same Jesus shall so come in like manner as ye have seen Him go into heaven." So sure were they that He would come soon that many of them sold their possessions, quit their jobs, and waited in prayer to greet Him upon His return.

But He didn't come during the lifetime of those disciples. He didn't come during the lifetime of the early church fathers, or of the Reformers, or of our fathers and grandfathers. Most of us don't really expect Him to come during our lifetime — certainly not today or tomorrow.

But just a minute. Is it really true that He has not come? A sudden heart attack, and for one more mortal man "the end of all things is at hand." The squeal of brakes applied a moment too late, and for a whole family "the end of all things is at hand." A sputtering in the airplane motor, and for perhaps 80 people "the end of all things is at hand."

Those early disciples were not really mistaken when they lived in the expectation of their Lord's early return. He did return to them — in many cases suddenly and soon — and when He returned it was, for each of them, one by one, the Last Judgment. He will come visibly on the Last Day, but He will also come again to every one of us — perhaps suddenly, certainly soon — and His coming will be our Last Judgment. And so we have good reason to be sober and to watch unto prayer, for we dare not face the Judge unless we can also greet Him as our Savior.

A Place Prepared

JOHN 14:1-6

One of the many titles by which the Christian is called in the Scriptures is "ambassador for Christ." It is a good title, for it expresses two profound truths about the Christian. On the one hand, it says that he has the high honor of being in this world on the King's business. On the other hand, it says that his assignment here is a temporary one — that someday he will be called home.

An ambassador cannot serve his king well if he hates the country to which he has been assigned and refuses to associate with its citizens. But he becomes a traitor to his king if he "goes native" and puts the interests of the country to which he has been sent above the interests of his home country.

We who are, at this moment in history, ambassadors from the heavenly court to this world need to cultivate the right kind of love for earth and its peoples. This is, after all, our Father's world in spite of all that sin and Satan have done to mar it; and we dishonor Him if we despise what

He has made. But we also need to keep reminding ourselves that earth is not our home, and even if our address were The White House or Buckingham Palace, it would not be our Father's house.

This means that we can enjoy everything that is good in this world, and yet feel that bittersweet tinge of homesickness which makes every ambassador look forward to the day when his assignment is finished and he can go home—home to the city fair and high, the mansion made ready for us, and the welcoming arms of the Father who is waiting for us there.

We See His Plan

LUKE 2:33-40

Few men have been blessed as was God's aged saint, Simeon. While "most men live lives of quiet desperation," Simeon knew what the purpose of his life was, for it had been revealed to him by the Holy Spirit that he should not die until he had seen the Messiah. And so, when Mary and Joseph brought the infant Jesus to the temple, Simeon could say with complete contentment and satisfaction, "Lord, now lettest Thou Thy servant depart in peace . . . for mine eyes have seen Thy salvation."

The wise men of our day tell us that the greatest single problem of modern man is the problem of meaninglessness. Why do we live? Why do we work? Why do we bear the heartaches and the pains that are the price of survival? What really stops us from taking the easy way out?

For many people, as for Hamlet, fear of what might lie beyond the grave makes suicide an unacceptable answer. Others solve the problem by getting so absorbed in a constant round of distractions that they never have to face up to the question of the meaning of it all. Still others manage, one way or another, to keep going even though they admit there is no good reason why they should.

But for Christian people, life has both meaning and purpose. In sorrow and in joy, in good times and bad, in triumphs and in failures we see God at work, accomplishing in us and in His world the salvation which His Son purchased for us. More than that, we have been given the high privilege of being His co-workers in this glorious undertaking. Therefore death, whether it come early or late, comes not as a horror or a tragedy but as a necessary step in the working-out of His gracious plan. Having seen in this life His salvation, we are ready to depart in peace so that He may show us those good things which eye hath not seen nor ear heard but which He has reserved for us in heaven.

Confident of God's Performance

PHILIPPIANS 1:3-11

Can I be sure of everlasting life?

There are good people who would answer: "No, I can hope for it and I can pray for it, but I can never be sure of it. To be sure of it would be presumptuous, and possibly even dangerous if my certainty tempted me to forget that I must fight the good fight. Doesn't the Bible itself say that I must work out my salvation with fear and trembling?"

It does indeed. Our Lord Himself speaks of striving to enter in at the strait gate, and He warns us that not everyone who says "Lord! Lord!" will enter into the kingdom of heaven, but only those who do the will of the Father in heaven. So how can I be sure that I will fight the good fight, strive to enter in at the strait gate, do the will of the Father, and work out my own salvation up to the very end of my life?

St. Paul's answer is: "If you are doing these things now, you are not doing them in your own strength or by your own decision. These are good works which God is doing in you, works which He began in you when He accepted you as His own in Baptism. Therefore, if you are tempted to fear that you might lose your faith, remember where it came from, remember your baptism. And then take comfort in the assurance that what God begins, He finishes. This is no mere pious hope. This is one thing of which you can be utterly confident."

And so my hope of everlasting life does not rest on any speculation about my own capacity to strive and to endure. It rests entirely on my confidence that the same God who called me as His own in Baptism will receive me as His own in the hour of my death.

This book has been set in Palatino (Linofilm),
printed on Warrens 66 Antique,
bound in Mead Mark I,
with graphics by Ken Paul.